kittenwar

kittenwar

FRASER LEWRY AND TOM RYAN

CHRONICLE BOOKS
SAN FRANCISCO

Library of Congress Cataloging-in-Publication Data:
Ryan, Tom
  Kittenwar / Tom Ryan & Fraser Lewry.
    p. cm.
ISBN-10: 0-8118-5980-0
ISBN-13: 978-0-8118-5980-6
1. Kittens—Miscellanea. 2. Kittens—Pictorial works.
I. Lewry, Fraser. II. Title.
  SF445.5.R93 2007
  636.8'07—dc22
  2006039214

Manufactured in China
Designed by Michael Morris

Distributed in Canada by Raincoast Books
9050 Shaughnessy Street
Vancouver, British Columbia V6P 6E5

10 9 8 7 6 5 4 3 2 1

Chronicle Books LLC
680 Second Street
San Francisco, California 94107
www.chroniclebooks.com

★ THE KITTENWAR STORY

Several years ago, I invented something.

It wasn't the kind of thing that really made a difference. It didn't cure disease or save fuel or keep your skin smooth, but it made people happy. I called it the Random Kitten Generator, and it was a Web page.

The premise was simple. Users were presented with a picture of a cute little kitten, beneath which sat a button reading, "Awwww. How cute! Show me another!" People would click on the button, whereupon another kitten would appear, as if by magic. Simple.

Word of my invention spread quickly to the fuzzier regions of the Internet. People used it by the millions.

And then I sold it. I was approached by a mysterious Ukrainian syndicate with a few dollars and a mysterious business plan; my resolve collapsed and I took the money. I wish I hadn't. They plastered the site with ads, and the magic vanished.

Wracked with guilt, I decided to build another site. This one would be bigger, better, and contain infinitely more kittens. Whereas the previous site had featured one kitten at a time, the new one would show two. Once this was settled, it seemed obvious to allow users to choose their favorite from each pairing. If they could do this, common sense dictated that I keep a tally of all the votes. I could then show the most cute and least cute kittens, and keep a running total of each feline's performance.

And thus, Kittenwar was born.

Except that it wasn't, not quite. Being personally incapable of programming my vision, I e-mailed Tom Ryan, fellow cat lover and coding wizard of the highest order. Tom didn't hesitate to come on board, and within days he was knee-deep in algorithms and formulae as we got the site off the ground.

Kittenwar.com went live in May 2005, and was an immediate success, before becoming an equally rapid failure. The amount of traffic we got crashed the server, taking the site offline, so we half-jokingly put a page online appealing for donations to buy our own, dedicated server.

Unbelievably, thrillingly, people responded. Within a fortnight we'd raised enough money to start afresh, and from that point we haven't looked back. Kittenwar has been on the front page of national news-papers, talked about on numerous radio and TV shows, and linked to from every conceivable kind of Web site. I even met a doctor who told me that the hospital she worked at relied on Kittenwar to keep the staff awake during marathon shifts (not while treating patients, I presume).

All of which brings us to what you're holding in your hands right now: the Kittenwar book. The result of many months of scientific research and impassioned debate, it brings you the battling thrill of Kittenwar without the need to crank up the computer, and adds plenty of brand-new, never-seen-before features.

Most important, however, it brings you kittens. Lots of kittens. Happy kittens. Playful kittens. Frisky kittens. Sharp-intake-of-breath-oh-my-god-he's-so-cute kittens. They're all here, and they'll make you feel good about life. In fact, research clearly demonstrates that if copies of this book were handed out to the leaders of warring nations, fighting would cease almost immediately. Go on, try it.

We hope you enjoy *Kittenwar*.

—FRASER LEWRY

★ TURN THE PAGE TO SEE THE WINNER!

S.

11

K.P.T.
PP. 44–45

CODE NAME:
★ HORACE

V

12

CODE NAME:
★ BOO

K.P.T.
PP.44–45

HOW TO READ
THIS BOOK

WHY DOES THIS BOOK NEED INSTRUCTIONS? Well, unlike titles such as *War and Peace* or *The Complete Works of Shakespeare*, in which readers simply turn the pages in numerical order until they reach the end, there is more than one way to read *Kittenwar*.

ONE CAN, IF ONE CHOOSES, READ *KITTENWAR* **IN THE TRADITIONAL MANNER,** slowly browsing through the pages, taking in everything *Kittenwar* has to offer: trivia, science, stories of strength and bravery, plus an enormous number of rather lovely pictures, as the Kittenwar soldiers go head-to-head.

Indeed, more conservative readers may feel more comfortable taking this classic approach. If this sounds like the kind of reading experience you'd enjoy, please start by turning to **page 10.**

THE MORE ADVENTUROUS, HOWEVER, MAY CHOOSE A DIFFERENT PATH, taking advantage of *Kittenwar*'s revolutionary use of book-construction technology. One of the unique features of this book is that the reader (that's you) can interact with the pages and, when faced with pairs of improbably cute kittens, do the impossible: choose the cutest.

Having done this, the reader (that's you again) can follow the instructions at the foot of the page and enter our highly innovative kittenological testing maze. Confused? Turn to **page 8** for further details.

★★★ **WHICHEVER METHOD YOU CHOOSE, SATISFACTION IS GUARANTEED.** ★★★

★ HOW TO USE OUR KITTENOLOGICAL PERSONALITY TEST

K.P.T.

LIKE TINY, FLUFFY BAROMETERS OF THE SOUL, particular types of kitten and our preferences for them reveal much about us as human beings. We have used this remarkable fact to turn our little book of kitten pictures into a cunning personality test, with results based on the decisions made by you, the reader.

Our highly trained team of cutting-edge kittenologists have combined their knowledge with the foremost psychonographers in the world today to create a unique and possibly award-winning system. All you need to do to find out all about yourself is follow our basic instructions. And remember: all this is achieved simply by looking at pictures of kittens.

HERE'S HOW TO USE OUR KITTEN-BASED PERSONALITY TESTER:

On the opposite page you'll see eight pictures of lovely kittens. Choose your favorite, look for this symbol **K.P.T.** , and turn to the pages indicated.

You'll be faced with two further pictures to choose from. Select the cutest, find the **K.P.T.** symbol below that kitten, and turn to the pages indicated. Repeat.

You might find that you see some kittens more than once. This means you're near the end of the test, but you need to reconsider some of your choices to get the correct result.

After you've looked at enough kittens, the book will direct you to the conclusion of the test, and our specially formulated, guaranteed 100% accurate*, scientifically verified results will inform you of what your choices revealed, and what they mean for you.

* May not actually be 100% accurate.

PRINCE

K.P.T.
PP.16–17

LEELU

K.P.T.
PP.20–21

PARIS

K.P.T.
PP.24–25

TENNA

K.P.T.
PP.14–15

TO START THE TEST, choose the cutest kitten and turn to the next page as instructed.

9

SMUDGEY

K.P.T.
PP.32–33

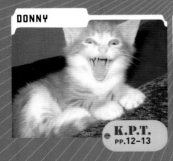

DONNY

K.P.T.
PP.12–13

CHARLIE

K.P.T.
PP.10–11

SPHYNXY

K.P.T.
PP.44–45

10

V

★ TURN THE PAGE TO SEE THE WINNER!

S.

13

K.P.T.
PP.42–43

CODE NAME:
★ BOBO

14

V

CODE NAME:
★ ELLA

K.P.T.
PP. 26–27

★ TURN THE PAGE TO SEE THE WINNER!

S.

15

K.P.T.
PP. 20-21

CODE NAME:
★ ZOD

16

V

CODE NAME:
★ OSCAR

K.P.T.
PP. 50–51

★TURN THE PAGE TO SEE THE WINNER!

S.

17

K.P.T.
PP.28–29

CODE NAME:
★ZIGGY

★ **ACCORDING TO**

53%

OF PEOPLE,
ZIGGY IS CUTER
THAN OSCAR.

ZIGGY

WELL DONE, ZIGGY!

OSCAR

★ PREPARING FOR KITTENWAR.

DO YOU WANT TO ENTER YOUR PET INTO KITTENWAR?

What's that? You do?

Remember, this is not a decision to be made lightly. What will happen if your kitten isn't as highly favored as you expect? Worse still, could you handle the rejection if he or she returned from battle alone and defeated, forced into submission by other supposedly cuter kittens? Could you cope?

You could? Then we'll start by making a comprehensive checklist. You'll need the following things:

1. A CAMERA
2. A KITTEN

And that's it. Forget all the stuff a so-called professional photographer would use. Lights? Not necessary. Expensive tripod? Waste of time. Glamorous assistant? Well, it'd be nice, but it's not absolutely compulsory.

All you really need are your wits and some patience. As anyone who's lived with cats will appreciate, getting them to perform to order is very difficult. A kitten might be naturally cute, but point a camera in its direction and there's every chance it'll scamper off and hide under a bed or wriggle beneath a pile of discarded cardboard boxes in the garage.

Patience is the key. With a digital camera, you can take hundreds of photos, and you might need them all to catch that one moment of unplanned, unparalleled, unbelievable cuteness.

THINGS NOT TO DO:

DON'T USE A FLASH. Kittens don't like it (does anyone?), and most likely, by the time you've decided that the shot wasn't good enough, little Felix will be nowhere to be seen.

DON'T FORCE THE ISSUE. Squeezing Timmy in to a sock because he'll look sweet wrapped in a purple wool tube simply won't work, because Timmy will get annoyed, try to scratch you, and refuse to cooperate further. Be patient, and eventually Timmy will do something spectacularly cute, without any help from you. Why? Because that's what he's good at. Just watch. Before you know it, he'll fall asleep in a saucer of milk or clamber into the bread box and start licking poppy seeds off a bagel, and only then will you have his blessing to take a picture. Timmy, you see, wants to look his best.

NO DOGS. Kittens might pretend to like dogs, but they're just humoring them.

And there you have it: the Kittenwar guide to capturing your cat at its cutest. If you adhere to these rules, there's no reason why you shouldn't produce a picture you can be rightly proud of and, more important, one that'll see your kitten triumph in battle.

MAY THE CUTEST KITTEN WIN.

V

★ BOB VS. ED

"BOB" AND "ED" ARE BOTH GOOD, SOLID, RELIABLE MONIKERS. If your real-life buddies had such names, tasks like cutting down a stubborn pine or fitting a new crankshaft would be easy. Need help with the barbecue? Hell, give Bob a call. Require a masonry bit for a power drill? It's likely that Ed has just what you need in his workshop.

BUT DOES THIS HELP US OUT when trying to separate kittens warring for cuteness? Probably not.

TAKE A LOOK AT PICTURE ONE. Bob's owner seems to be suffering from some kind of knee injury, but he's happy to let Bob clamber up over his protective brace, ignoring the vague possibility of further damage. This demonstrates a great degree of trust between pet and owner, a feeling reflected in Bob's face. He's a little concerned that his owner isn't as mobile as he was before the injury, and those wide eyes seem to be begging for a quick return to health. Bob wants to play, but Bob will have to wait. It's this unspoken sadness that makes him so cute, alongside those brilliant blue eyes and soft ginger fur.

SO HOW CAN ED COMPETE? He starts off well, being splendidly, naturally cute, and scores points for walking with what appears to be a slightly unsteady gait. This trait, popular among the very youngest kittens, almost always adds to their appeal. A kitten that struggles to stand, as if it's been at the bar all night with Pete and Dave and Al, sinking cans of Coors and discussing football, is a very attractive kitten indeed.

WHAT ED MISSES OUT ON IS PROPS. While Bob has an injured owner and an imploring look that tugs at our heartstrings, Ed hasn't prepared for his photo shoot in the same way. He's relied on little more than his inherent cuteness to win favor, and while this might be enough to defeat many other kittens on the battlefield, Bob's brilliant, innovative use of a medical support sees him triumph.

24

V

★ TURN THE PAGE TO SEE THE WINNER!

S.

25

K.P.T.
PP. 50–51

CODE NAME:
★ OSCAR

V

26

CODE NAME:
★ **MOOCH**

K.P.T.
PP. 58–59

★ TURN THE PAGE TO SEE THE WINNER!

S.

27

K.P.T.
PP.56–57

CODE NAME:
★ELLIE

28

V

CODE NAME:

★ BOLLY

K.P.T.
PP. 46–47

★ TURN THE PAGE TO SEE THE WINNER!

S.

29

K.P.T.
PP.56–57

CODE NAME:
★ CANDY CLAWS

BATTLE RESULTS

★ **IT TURNS OUT THAT**

56%

OF PEOPLE THINK THAT BOLLY IS CUTER THAN CANDY CLAWS.

BOLLY

WELL DONE, BOLLY!

CANDY CLAWS

BOLLY VS. CANDY CLAWS

TWO KITTENS, BOTH TERRIBLY CUTE, YET ONE SLIGHTLY MORE POPULAR. WHY? LET'S EXAMINE THE EVIDENCE.

BOLLY APPEARS TO BE WEDGED INTO A WASTEBASKET. What's more, she looks a little surprised to be there. This kind of innocence, this "wait a minute—a few seconds ago I was asleep by the fire, and now I've been upended and am lying on top of an old newspaper and a discarded banana peel while someone points a camera at me" kind of indignation, is actually quite endearing to us humans.

Bolly looks a little nonplussed, but she doesn't look upset, and this is important. A degree of trust is obviously present between her and whoever's behind the lens, so while she may look startled, she doesn't appear to be scared.

CANDY CLAWS, ON THE OTHER HAND, looks completely at home, with not a care in the world apart from whether it's tuna or chicken for dinner. Obviously comfortable in the company of her human, she's got a loving look in her eye that we generally find most alluring. She also looks a little younger than Bolly, which is normally a crucial advantage in any serious battle for cuteness supremacy.

THE SCORES, HOWEVER, TELL A DIFFERENT STORY. Little Candy Claws may have a slight advantage in terms of the very basic levels of cuteness, but Bolly still scores more strongly. Why? Is it the trash can? The casual observer would assume so, but an expert will have spotted the reason straightaway: the markings on Candy Claws' fur. She has the spotted markings of a leopard, and while we find this attractive at a superficial level, we have a deep-rooted, subconscious fear of the unknown, of being alone and vulnerable in the wild, of noises in the dark. Well, let's just say we're afraid that Candy Claws will rip out our throats and feast on our still-warm flesh before spending the afternoon chasing wildebeest across the Serengeti. You never know. It could happen.

V

★ TURN THE PAGE TO SEE THE WINNER!

S.

33

K.P.T.
PP. 38–39

CODE NAME:
★ WUSSY

34

V

CODE NAME:
★ **SOURIS**

K.P.T.
PP.38–39

S.

35

K.P.T.
PP.62–63

CODE NAME:
★ SHOUTY

BATTLE RESULTS

★**OVER**

52%

THINK THAT SHOUTY IS CUTER THAN SOURIS.

SHOUTY

FANTASTIC, SHOUTY!

SOURIS

★ KITTEN HEROES, PART ONE:
GREAT JOURNEYS

KITTENS MAY BE CUTE, BUT THEY CAN ENDURE THE TOUGHEST HARDSHIPS.

TAKE SIX-WEEK-OLD VILLY, FOR INSTANCE. He survived a sixteen-day transatlantic journey in a shipping container after sneaking aboard a freighter in Canada. Little Villy traveled 2,500 miles to Tamworth, in the United Kingdom, before being found by workers in a carpet warehouse. Vets think that Villy, named after racing driver Jacques Villeneuve, survived by licking moisture off the container's walls.

EVEN REAL WAR PRODUCES FELINE HEROES. Fed up with all that nasty noise during the Iraq War, super-kitten Gracie crept into a tank near Baghdad and emerged six weeks later when the armored vehicle arrived back in England. Gracie survived the traumatic trip by eating bugs, and she was so tiny on arrival that she had to be fed with a syringe. She survived.

IT DOESN'T STOP THERE. Staff at a furniture store in Salisbury, England, were startled to find an eight-week-old kitten in a delivery from Penang, in Malaysia. Little Flowerpot, as she became known, had survived for more than a month at sea without food.

THESE KITTENS ARE HEROES. WE SALUTE THEM.

38

V

★ TURN THE PAGE TO SEE THE WINNER!

S.

39

K.P.T.
PP. 74–75

CODE NAME:
★ MIAH

★ THE RESULTS ARE IN:

62%

OF PEOPLE THINK THAT FRITO IS CUTER THAN MIAH.

40

FRITO

GOOD SHOW, FRITO!

MIAH

★ FRITO VS. MIAH

TO THE UNTRAINED OBSERVER, this statistic is an absolute anomaly. Why do so many people consider Frito cuter than Miah? Surely they're equally delightful, no? Both are tiny, delicious bundles of fluff, sharing all of the most captivating traits of genuine feline appeal. Big eyes? Check. Oversize ears? Check. Innocence? Check. Vulnerability? Check. If anything, Miah appears to be slightly smaller than Frito, which should add to her appeal.

SO WHY THE DIFFERENCE? THANKFULLY, ANY WELL-TRAINED KITTEN-OLOGIST WILL BE ABLE TO PROVIDE AN ANSWER.

It's all about being ginger. While some humans tend to think of people with orange hair as being slightly inferior to the rest of mankind, the opposite is true of kittens, for whom being ginger is akin to being born to millionaire parents, or into a family of great athletes. While a ginger kitten may not have any obvious physical advantages, its breeding sets that kitty up for life in a way that no amount of schooling ever can.

The kind of confidence instilled by being ginger is therefore reflected in the scoring of this battle. Subconsciously, we're thinking, "These kittens are both extremely cute, but I better vote for the ginger one in case he becomes president one day."

Having said that, we think Miah would make an adorable secretary of state.

42

V

S.

43

K.P.T.
PP.64–65

CODE NAME:
★ DOUBLE WHISKEY

44

V

CODE NAME:
★ BIANCA

K.P.T.
PP. 72–73

S.

45

K.P.T.
PP.70–71

CODE NAME:
★ ASLAN

V

46

CODE NAME:
★ LOKI

K.P.T.
PP. 66–67

★ TURN THE PAGE TO SEE THE WINNER!

S.

K.P.T.
PP.72–73

CODE NAME:
★ BUTTONS

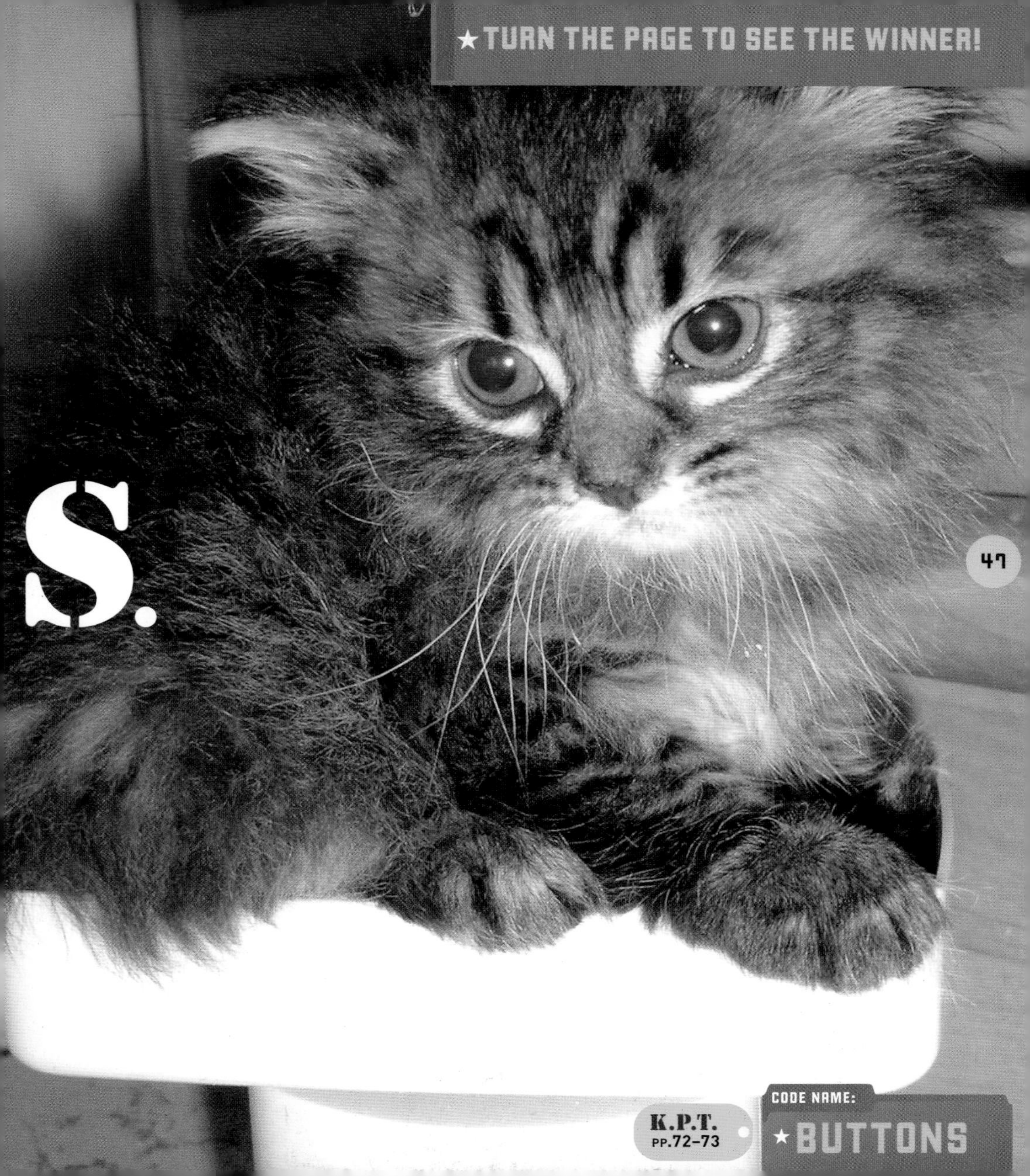

★IT'S A DRAW!
LOKI AND BUTTONS
BOTH WIN

50%

OF THE TIME.

48

LOKI

BRILLIANT!

BUTTONS

★ KITTEN CENSUS

Kittenwar.com has carried out the world's most comprehensive survey ever on cat names, questioning more than 100,000 kitten owners from across the globe to discover the most popular names for our feline friends.

HERE, IN ORDER, ARE THE TOP 50 KITTEN NAMES:

1. Molly
2. Max
3. Zoe
4. Oscar
5. Charlie
6. Kitty
7. Chloe
8. Gizmo
9. Tigger
10. Lily
11. Sophie
12. Lucy
13. Bella
14. Jack
15. Simba
16. Milo
17. Oliver
18. Smokey
19. Loki
20. Angel
21. Tiger
22. Luna
23. Bailey
24. Smudge
25. Maggie
26. Lola
27. Rocky
28. Daisy
29. Shadow
30. Toby
31. Misty
32. Leo
33. Jasper
34. Mia
35. Spike
36. Sasha
37. Willow
38. Princess
39. Coco
40. Pepper
41. Cleo
42. Oreo
43. Missy
44. George
45. Ginger
46. Mimi
47. Pumpkin
48. Phoebe
49. Sammy
50. Gracie

V

★ TURN THE PAGE TO SEE THE WINNER!

S.

51

K.P.T.
PP.86–87

CODE NAME:
★ MILO

52

V

CODE NAME:
★ NIJNTJE

K.P.T.
PP. 62–63

★ TURN THE PAGE TO SEE THE WINNER!

S.

53

K.P.T. PP.70–71

CODE NAME:
★ PARSLEY

BATTLE RESULTS

★ OUR RESEARCH
SHOWS THAT:

65 %

NIJNTJE

CHEERS, NIJNTJE!

OF PEOPLE THINK
THAT NIJNTJE IS
CUTER THAN
PARSLEY.

PARSLEY

★ NIJNTJE VS. PARSLEY

"NIJNTJE" IS A VERY STRANGE NAME FOR A KITTEN. We're not even sure how to pronounce it. "Nidge-nit-jey?" It doesn't roll off the tongue very naturally, but that's because Nijntje is Dutch, and the only people who can speak Dutch without sounding like their throats are attempting to arm-wrestle their tongues are the Dutch themselves. Luckily, we found ourselves a Dutchman, who patiently explained that the name Nijntje is based on the way a Dutch child might mispronounce *konijntje*, which means "little rabbit." How lovely.

"PARSLEY," HOWEVER, IS A MUCH MORE COMMON NAME for a kitten. In fact, parsley is the only herb that's commonly used as a cat name. When was the last time you met a kitty called Turmeric? Or Chives? Or Bolivian Coriander? See what we mean?

SO WHY DO PEOPLE PREFER THE LITTLE RABBIT TO PARSLEY? In this case, it's all about the pose. Check out Nijntje, spread-eagled on the floor, belly exposed for all the world to rub. This posture suggests a great happiness, and a trust in those in the room, both cat and human. We're immediately drawn to this pose, its innocence reflected in our own senti-mental reaction.

PARSLEY, HOWEVER, IS ATTACKING A LAPTOP WITH GREAT GUSTO, and our thoughts immediately turn to insurance. Is our policy up-to-date? Does this count as accidental damage, or as an act of God? Where did I leave the paperwork? Have I paid the premiums this month?

PARSLEY'S VIOLENT REACTION TO TECHNOLOGY means that only the most well-covered will immediately concern themselves with her cuteness. The rest of us will skip quickly back to Nijntje, place our vote, and be gone.

V

S.

57

K.P.T.
PP.78–79

CODE NAME:
★TENNESSEE

V

58

CODE NAME:
★ PIPPIN

K.P.T.
PP.92–93

★ TURN THE PAGE TO SEE THE WINNER!

S.

59

K.P.T.
PP.84–85

CODE NAME:
★ KENSOU

★ PIPPIN WINS KITTENBATTLES AGAINST KENSOU

53%

OF THE TIME.

PIPPIN

PIPPIN VICTORIOUS!

KENSOU

KITTEN HEROES, PART TWO:
BRAVERY

KITTENS MAY BE CUTE, BUT THEY HAVE THE HEARTS OF LIONS.

A PERFECT EXAMPLE IS TWELVE-WEEK-OLD SYLVESTER, who climbed into a washing machine, unnoticed by owner Bianca Marten, just before the machine was switched on. After spending twenty minutes in the scorching hot water, Sylvester was finally rescued, dizzy but alive. Bianca immediately rushed the little kitten to the vet, where he was declared fit and returned home. Confronting his fears, Sylvester straightaway climbed back into the machine.

IT'S COMMON KNOWLEDGE THAT CATS AND KITTENS DON'T USUALLY LIKE WATER, which makes the story of our next kitten all the more remarkable. A group of friends fishing three miles out in the Gulf of Mexico spotted something odd in the water and turned their boat around to investigate. The tiny package turned out to be an apricot-colored kitten, paddling desperately, quite plainly terrified, but determined to survive. It's unclear how the castaway got to be so far from shore, but he was rescued and given a clean bill of health, and is happy in a new home, with a new name: Nemo.

SPEEDY THE KITTEN IS AN INTERNET LEGEND. The son of a stray cat in Millersville, Pennsylvania, Speedy was born without a pelvis and was unable to walk, so a local veterinarian built a cart out of kids' toys to support his back legs. Within a day, Speedy had mastered his new wheels and was busily whizzing around, doing the kind of things that happy little cats do.

THESE KITTENS ARE HEROES. WE SALUTE THEM.

62

V

★ TURN THE PAGE TO SEE THE WINNER!

S.

63

K.P.T.
PP.86–87

CODE NAME:
★ TOM

TOM WINS: 55%

V

64

CODE NAME:
★ POOKIE

● K.P.T.
PP. 90–91

★ TURN THE PAGE TO SEE THE WINNER!

S.

65

K.P.T. PP.88–89 CODE NAME: ★YODA

V

66

CODE NAME:

★ PRECH

K.P.T.
PP. 72–73

★ TURN THE PAGE TO SEE THE WINNER!

S.

67

K.P.T.
PP. 74–75

CODE NAME:
★ZEKE

BATTLE RESULTS

★ **BELIEVE IT OR NOT,**

53%

OF PEOPLE THINK THAT PRECH IS CUTER THAN ZEKE.

PRECH

CONGRATS, PRECH!

ZEKE

PRECH VS. ZEKE

★

IT'S ONE OF THE GREAT CAT CONUNDRUMS: many love to sit or sleep in sinks, baths, and basins, despite an innate fear of water. They love the feel of cool porcelain against their fur, yet the proximity of their liquid nemesis doesn't seem to faze them at all. Why?

To be honest, we have no idea. Anyway, on with the battle.

PRECH AND ZEKE are both enchanting examples of kitten-kind. They could even be brothers—both are tabbies with distinctive "M" forehead markings; both are of a similar size and shape—yet Prech holds sway in the contest for cuteness. This is despite him looking bored in his photograph, a most unkittenlike state of affairs. His expression says, "Is that all you've got? I'm really not impressed," whereas most kittens are excited by everything around them, even the stuff they were playing with a couple of minutes ago. This suggests that Prech has a mighty intellect, which is somewhat unusual in a feline, can be something to fear, and counts against him when considering cuteness. After all, who would you rather vote for: a kitten who, when coming across a ball of yarn, thinks, "Wow! I can have a brilliant fight with this" or one who moves on sedately after wondering whether it's made of natural or synthetic fibers?

ZEKE, however, suffers from a much more serious vulnerability: he's wet. This is such an unnatural state of affairs for a kitten that our instinct is to recoil, fearing that some kind of primitive cruelty has taken place. Of course, that is very unlikely. It's much more plausible that Zeke has been out chasing squirrels, and his kindly owner has taken the time to wash some of the more steadfast grime from Zeke's fur. For his part, Zeke, while not being completely comfortable with the experience, does appreciate the gesture.

Although he's still really annoyed about being beaten by Prech.

70

V

CODE NAME:
★GIZMO

K.P.T.
PP.96–97

★ TURN THE PAGE TO SEE THE WINNER!

S.

71

K.P.T.
PP. 80–81

CODE NAME:
★ JOSEPHINE

72

V

CODE NAME:
★ SMUDGE

● K.P.T.
PP.98–99

★ TURN THE PAGE TO SEE THE WINNER!

S.

73

K.P.T.
PP.96–97

CODE NAME:
★ SIMBA

V

74

CODE NAME:
★ NEKO BURRITO POTATO CHIP

K.P.T.
PP.104–105

★TURN THE PAGE TO SEE THE WINNER!

S.

75

K.P.T.
PP. 80–81

CODE NAME:
★PERCIVAL

BATTLE RESULTS

★ **POOR NEKO BURRITO POTATO CHIP LOSES TO PERCIVAL**

66%

OF THE TIME.

NEKO BURRITO POTATO CHIP

PERCIVAL PREVAILS!

PERCIVAL

★ THE SCIENCE OF KITTENOLOGY

THE THEORY OF CUTENESS

IT HAS LONG BEEN RECOGNIZED that the juvenile form of *Felis sylvestris catus* is the most adorable animal on the face of the earth, and that anyone seeking to counter this claim is obviously foolish, quite possibly mad, and most likely dangerous.

Indeed, since the very beginning of time, man has been rendered completely insensible in the presence of kittens. Understanding the nature of this power is key to our worldview: there's no point in being able to explain ten-dimensional string theory (go on, look it up) if science fails to fathom why grown, tough men like lumberjacks and bricklayers make cooing noises when confronted with a two-month-old kitten.

THE SEARCH FOR KNOWLEDGE

PHYSICIST SIR ISAAC NEWTON (who invented gravity during tests to discover why cats, when dropped, always land on their feet) was a great cat lover, and he has even been credited with the invention of the cat flap; while he was conducting experiments with prisms in the dark, his kitten was able to come and go through a small, specially made felt-covered opening in his door. Newton did not reach any solid conclusions on the science behind feline charm, but his research into light and gravity did enable later students to begin the serious business of assembling a deeper understanding of the subject.

Biologists, meanwhile, have not been so successful. Laboratory attempts to isolate the cuteness gene have traditionally been thwarted by the escape of the test kittens and the subsequent havoc created among the lab's other residents, rats and mice. In a nutshell, cats and biology simply don't mix.

A BREAKTHROUGH

A MAJOR RECENT BREAKTHROUGH in cuteness theory came in the field of pure mathematics, building on the work of physicists like Newton. Unfortunately, the solution offered was so incomprehensibly, mind-numbingly complex that everyone involved got bored really quickly and went back to playing with the kittens instead. We can exclusively reveal, however, that it has something to do with the size of the eyes in relation to the head. Or it could involve whiskers. We're not quite sure, as we weren't really paying attention either.

V

K.P.T.
PP.122–123

★ TURN THE PAGE TO SEE THE WINNER!

S.

79

K.P.T.
PP.120–121

CODE NAME:
★ OBES

OBES WINS: 65%

80

V

CODE NAME:

★TALLULAH

K.P.T.
PP.98–99

S.

81

CODE NAME:
★ ADMIRAL JUDAH

BATTLE RESULTS

★ IT'S CLOSE, BUT

53 %

OF PEOPLE THINK THAT **TALLULAH** IS CUTER THAN **ADMIRAL JUDAH.**

TALLULAH

CHEERS, TALLULAH!

ADMIRAL JUDAH

TALLULAH VS. ADMIRAL JUDAH

FOR A MOMENT, before we consider these statistics, let's take stock:

FACT 1: All kittens are beautiful.

FACT 2: This includes the ones that look a bit weird.

TAKEN AT FACE VALUE, both these heavenly creatures might seem to be a little unusual. Tallulah appears to have fine pink fur and orange eyes, while Admiral Judah is partially hairless. These kinds of kittens tend to fill up the "losingest" list on our Web site, consistently beaten into second place by a barrage of more "normal" tabbies and torties, and it makes us angry. Furious, in fact.

DID THE CIVIL RIGHTS MOVEMENT ACHIEVE NOTHING? Are we still intolerant of those whose physical appearance places them in a minority? This is the twenty-first century. Haven't we moved on? It appears not.

SO IT'S TIME FOR CHANGE. It's time once again to march on the capital, time to raise our banners high and proclaim, "No more! Equality for all!" and not to rest until we're living in a world where Tallulah and Admiral Judah can be judged fairly, where their outward appearance won't prompt people to point and snigger and leer and ridicule. It's time to fight for their rights.

UNTIL WE REACH THAT STAGE, though, Tallulah is cuter than Admiral Judah because she simply looks less weird.

FACT 3: Both Tallulah and Admiral Judah are still beautiful.

V

CODE NAME:
★ FREDDIE

K.P.T.
PP.128–129

S.

K.P.T.
PP.106–107

CODE NAME:
★ NEMO

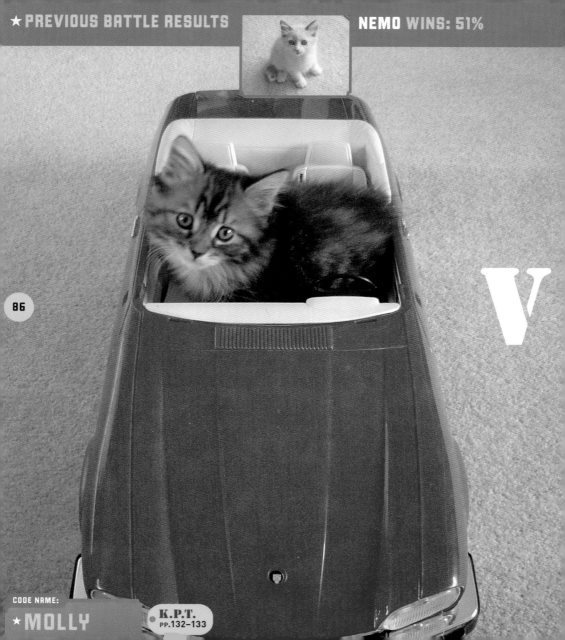

86

V

K.P.T.
PP.132–133

★ TURN THE PAGE TO SEE THE WINNER!

S.

87

K.P.T.
PP.110–111

CODE NAME:
★ OSCAR

V

88

★ TURN THE PAGE TO SEE THE WINNER!

S.

89

K.P.T.
PP.114–115

CODE NAME:
★ GABBY

V

90

CODE NAME:
★ WHISPER

K.P.T.
PP. 106–107

S.

91

K.P.T.
PP.120–121

CODE NAME:
★KINKY

92

S.

93

K.P.T.
PP.100–101

CODE NAME:
★CHLOE

★ **THE RESULTS ARE IN, AND**

69%

SWITCH

WELL DONE, SWITCH!

CHLOE

OF PEOPLE THINK THAT SWITCH IS CUTER THAN CHLOE.

94

SWITCH VS. CHLOE

LET'S FACE IT: IT'S OBVIOUS. While both kittens are infused with record-breaking amounts of animal magnetism, it's Switch who is far more comfortable under the camera's steely gaze.

CHLOE HAS OBVIOUSLY BEEN SURPRISED BY THE PHOTOGRAPHER, caught unawares during post-meal cleanup. It's a beginner's mistake, and one she'll make less frequently as time passes and she becomes used to all the attention. Those few remaining crumbs of tuna may taste delicious, but they don't make for the most flattering portrait.

SWITCH, ON THE OTHER HAND, IS A PROFESSIONAL. Every inch of her tiny being is projecting toward the lens. Notice the way she coyly ducks her head into the pillow? This is precisely the same technique used by the late Princess Diana, a trick that saw her flourish as one of the world's most glamorous women.

Then there's the way Switch bashfully pulls the bedding toward her, as if to preserve her modesty, yet at the same time hinting at something tantalizing lying beneath. She is working her body, the lens, and us.

Finally, she's had the sense to be photographed in surroundings that match those brilliant blue eyes. This final piece of stage management completes an outrageously pretty picture.

SWITCH MAY BE YOUNG, but she's the ultimate professional. Chloe has much to learn.

v

CODE NAME:

★ GUS

K.P.T.
PP.100–101

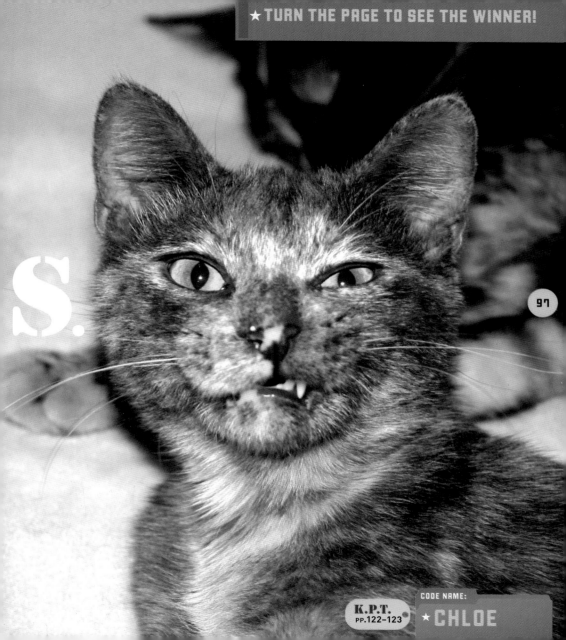

★ TURN THE PAGE TO SEE THE WINNER!

S.

97

K.P.T.
PP.122–123

CODE NAME:
★ CHLOE

98

V

CODE NAME:
★ CALLIE

K.P.T.
PP.114–115

★ TURN THE PAGE TO SEE THE WINNER!

S.

99

K.P.T.
PP.128–129

CODE NAME:
★ LINUS

V

100

CODE NAME:
★ COPITO

K.P.T.
PP.134–135

★ TURN THE PAGE TO SEE THE WINNER!

S.

101

CODE NAME:
★ FANNY

★ **THESE KITTENS ARE VERY SIMILAR, BUT**

55%

COPITO

FANNY

FANNY TRIUMPHANT!

OF PEOPLE THINK THAT FANNY IS CUTER THAN COPITO.

★ COPITO VS. FANNY

LOOK AT THESE TWO: THEY COULD BE TWINS. Both are deliriously lovely bundles of delicious white fuzz, each infused with ludicrous amounts of kitty-cuteness. So why does little Copito come off second best?

LET'S START WITH FANNY. She looks content. Her owner obviously gives her full access to the kitchen, where she's allowed to patrol the work surfaces, stopping only to examine fruit or pick at saucers laden with fresh salmon. She's happy in this environment, and this comes across in her relaxed pose. We humans envy this carefree existence, where Fanny's only concern is how to reach the floor without knocking over the ironing, and we vote accordingly.

WITH COPITO, however, more sinister forces are at work. First, Copito has the name of a Mafia hit man, and this makes us wary. There's not a cat owner in the land who wants to call their pet in for dinner, only to be caught in the crossfire of a hail of bullets shot in retribution for the time that Freddie Four-Paws messed with Tony the Fur. Second, and most disturbingly, his photograph reveals a distressing fact: Copito appears to dwell in someone's hair. Who is it? One of his victims? We'll probably never know.

COPITO TERRIFIES US, which is why he scores less favorably. This is the dark side of kittendom, something we rarely get to see. We should all be grateful for that.

104

V

★ TURN THE PAGE TO SEE THE WINNER!

S.

105

K.P.T.
PP.132–133

CODE NAME:
★ MITZY

V

CODE NAME:
★ MAX I

K.P.T.
PP.78–79

★TURN THE PAGE TO SEE THE WINNER!

S.

107

K.P.T.
PG.154

CODE NAME:
★ALFIE

★ ALFIE WINS

62 %

OF THE TIME AGAINST MAX I.

MAX I

ALFIE

CHEERS, ALFIE!

★ TEN REASONS WHY CATS ARE CUTER THAN HUMANS.

1. **A CAT CAN TURN ITS EARS** 180 degrees. Most humans can't even twitch theirs.

2. **CATS CAN SEE** about six times better than humans in the dark. This is why they're much better at hunting at night. We need flashlights; cats don't. This also saves on batteries.

3. **A CAT CAN USE BARBS** on its tongue to scoop up water when it drinks. Go on, you try it.

4. **CATS SPEND ABOUT 30%** of their lives grooming themselves. Some humans don't even take a shower in the morning.

5. **SCIENTISTS HAVE PROVED** that stroking a cat can lower a human's blood pressure. Try the same on another human and you'll most likely end up in court.

6. **AFTER BEING WOKEN UP,** a cat becomes alert faster than any other animal. Some humans, on the other hand, can sleep through a series of alarms, arriving at the office much later than they should, flustered and pretending that their house had been broken into, or a drain had burst, or describing how Mr. Hedges across the street had parked his car in front of their driveway. If this behavior persists, humans are in danger of losing their job. Certainly, a disciplinary hearing is inevitable. This would never happen to a cat.

7. **A CAT CAN JUMP** five times its own height. If humans could do this, we could clear two London double-decker buses stacked one on top of the other. But we can't, which is probably a good thing. Imagine the injuries on landing.

8. **WHILE HUMANS HAVE** 206 bones in their bodies, cats have 230. This must be useful for something.

9. **EACH YEAR,** Americans spend a billion dollars more on cat food than they do on baby food. This means that cats are more important to the economy than humans. Or something like that. We're not quite sure. We're not economists.

10. **CATS CAN REACH SPEEDS** of 31 miles per hour when running. Even the fastest humans can barely hit 26 miles per hour. To demonstrate this using a real-life example: a cat, running flat out, could get from New York to Chicago in about 26 hours, while a human would still be 5 hours away on Interstate 90.

110

V

★ TURN THE PAGE TO SEE THE WINNER!

S.

111

K.P.T.
PG.155

CODE NAME:
★ FRANKIE

★ IT'S CLOSE, BUT FRANKIE WINS

51%

OF THE TIME AGAINST SYKSY.

SYKSY

FRANKIE

CHEERS, FRANKIE!

★KITTEN HEROES, PART THREE:
LIFE SAVERS

KITTENS MAY BE CUTE, BUT THEY CAN ALSO BE THE DIFFERENCE BETWEEN LIFE AND DEATH.

SOME CATS ARE TREATED SO BADLY AS KITTENS, it's a wonder they have any time for humans at all. Take Tee Cee, for example, tossed in a river and left for dead as a youngster. Instead of abandoning mankind altogether, Tee Cee has learned to recognize when his new owner, Michael Edmonds, is about to have an epileptic fit. Tee Cee stares intently at Michael just prior to his fits, as if picking up some unseen warning, then runs to Michael's wife, Jean, to attract her attention. Once assistance has arrived, Tee Cee refuses to leave his master's side until Michael regains consciousness.

ANOTHER CAT CAPABLE OF SAVING LIVES IS YOUNG COFFEE, who alerted his sleeping master, John Chislett, to a potentially deadly kitchen fire by biting him on the nose and batting him until he awoke, despite suffering from smoke inhalation. Both man and cat survived their ordeal.

THE LAST THING YOU EXPECT to find in your garden is a deadly Eastern Cottonmouth snake, especially if you live in Quebec, but that is exactly what confronted Kimberley Kotar. With the snake obviously upset and only inches away, Kimberley feared the worst until her cat, Sosa, leapt to her protection, striking out at the hissing serpent and receiving a bite to her paw. With no cottonmouth serum available in the province, Kimberley might not have survived, but brave little Sosa recovered after a mere three days' illness.

THESE KITTENS ARE HEROES. WE SALUTE THEM.

114

V

S.

115

K.P.T.
PG. 156

CODE NAME:
★ SAMSON

V

116

CODE NAME:
★TONTO

K.P.T.
PP.138–139

★ TURN THE PAGE TO SEE THE WINNER!

S.

117

K.P.T.
PP.122–123

CODE NAME:
★ BENNIFER

BATTLE RESULTS

★ **OUR SURVEY REVEALS THAT**

54%

OF PEOPLE THINK THAT BENNIFER IS CUTER THAN TONTO.

BENNIFER

BRAVO BENNIFER!

TONTO

★ BENNIFER VS. TONTO

ONE OF THE MOST CURIOUS LESSONS we've learned from Kittenwar is

that people love to see animals doing the kind of things that humans do. Whether it's as simple as a favorite pet standing on its hind legs to reach a dangling treat or a kitten that's actually taught itself to drive (see page 86), we love kittens that remind us of ourselves.

But how does that apply here? At first glance both kittens appear to be acting out normal, kitteny roles. Tonto looks a little disgruntled at having to sleep in a bed that's slightly smaller than her tiny frame, whereas Bennifer isn't really doing much, apart from looking a bit puzzled and hopelessly cute.

SO WHY DOES BENNIFER TRIUMPH? Some of the most experienced pro-

fessional kitten-watchers have struggled to identify the reason for this, but we can now reveal the secret to Bennifer's success: glamour.

NOT ONLY does Bennifer have one of those hybrid Hollywood couple names

(Bennifer = Ben Affleck + Jennifer Lopez) that are all the rage with those obsessed with celebrity, but examination of her picture reveals even closer ties with the rich and famous. See the paperwork that Bennifer is taking a break from? It appears that she is organizing a party, and quite a swanky one at that. And let's face it: what kind of party would be organized by a kitten with a network of contacts in show business? The best party *ever*, we suspect. Stars and starlets would mingle, then everyone would chase stuff around the garden before falling asleep in a big pile.

SO HOWEVER CUTE WE FIND TONTO to be (which is extremely cute

indeed), what we really want is to be part of Bennifer's world. And who can blame us?

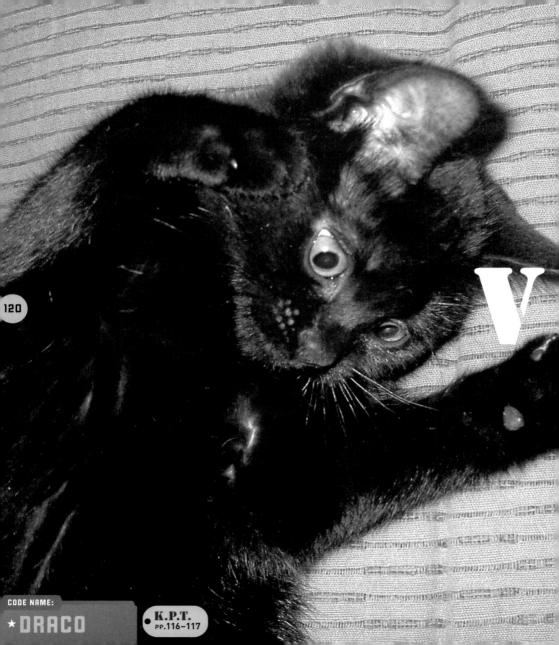

V

S.

121

K.P.T.
PG.157

CODE NAME:
★ SOPHIE

122

V

CODE NAME:
★ BIBI

K.P.T.
PP.90–91

S.

123

K.P.T.
PG.150

CODE NAME:
★GEMMA

124

V

S.

125

CODE NAME:
★ AMILIA

★IT'S OFFICIAL:

55%

OF PEOPLE THINK THAT HONEY BEE IS CUTER THAN AMILIA.

HONEY BEE

WELL DONE, HONEY BEE!

AMILIA

HONEY BEE VS. AMILIA

NORMALLY WE DON'T ALLOW other types of animals into Kittenwar, so we're not quite sure what happened with Amilia. Perhaps we initially mistook her bunny buddy for some kind of child's toy, or perhaps a nice plump cushion.

Either way, the presence of a rabbit in the shot should not detract from Amilia's very obvious cuteness. In fact, the friendship between the two animals only serves to enhance the charm of the pose: two creatures from completely different species presenting a degree of togetherness beyond the reach of us humans. Indeed, mankind has much to learn from the example set by Amilia, especially before we go on to colonize other planets.

AND YET, HONEY BEE TRIUMPHS. There she sits, performing what looks to be a most unladylike Heimlich maneuver on herself, but she outscores Amilia.

Why? Well, it's a combination of factors. First of all, there's no denying that Honey Bee is a particularly cute kitten. Calico cats tend to do very well in Kittenwar (perhaps it's the natural camouflage), but she also has the bright eyes and glossy coat of a true champion. Plus, she's clever enough to expose the pads of her feet for the photographer, something we humans find very seductive. Finally, and most controversially, Honey Bee has chosen a very cute name for herself. Selecting a title more normally associated with a smaller animal is a sure way to gain votes, especially when the animal in question is also cute. (And let's face it, bees are rather nice. They have yellow stripes and they're fuzzy. We like them. Well, apart from killer bees. Those are nasty.)

TO DEMONSTRATE THIS THEORY IN REAL LIFE, we took two newborn identical twin kittens, naming one Butterfly and the other Goat. After six months of people deciding who was cutest, we compiled all the statistics into a spreadsheet and examined the results.

We think you can probably guess who won.

V

CODE NAME:
★ BOFFERDING

K.P.T.
PP. 140–141

★ TURN THE PAGE TO SEE THE WINNER!

S.

129

K.P.T.
PP.122–123

CODE NAME:
★ MILLYMOLLYMANDY

★ **BOFFERDING WINS**

66%

OF HIS BATTLES AGAINST MILLY-MOLLYMANDY.

130

BOFFERDING

CONGRATS, BOFFERDING!

MILLYMOLLYMANDY

★ THE KITTENWAR GLOBAL CUTENESS SURVEY

OUR UNRIVALED DATABASE OF KITTEN CUTENESS is based on millions of kitten battles judged by hundreds of thousands of people from countries all over the world. Through a combined use of state-of-the-art network tracing technology and the most advanced geolocation systems available, the vast repository of kitten-related data on Kittenwar.com has been analyzed to compile a definitive survey of the countries of origin of the cutest kittens from around the globe.

WE INVITED THE FINEST STATISTICIANS to join us in our orbiting Kittenwar HQ, where we processed our data using the world's most powerful super-computers to produce the ultimate global cuteness index. The result of our labor was an unparalleled snapshot of the adorability of the world's fluffiest inhabitants—supremely detailed, incomparably accurate, a true milestone of statistical kittenology.

UNFORTUNATELY, one of the authors left most of the report on a bus, and all we have left is a list of the top ten cutest kitten nationalities. Here it is:

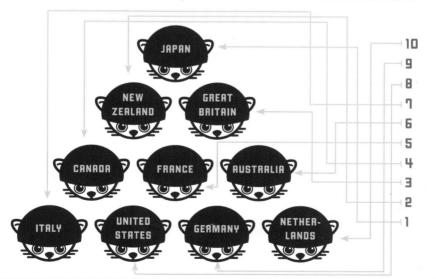

V

CODE NAME:
★BUSTER

K.P.T.
PP.142–143

S.

133

CODE NAME:
★NINJA

134

V

CODE NAME:
★ **SCOUT**

K.P.T.
PP.104–105

★ TURN THE PAGE TO SEE THE WINNER!

S.

135

K.P.T.
PG.152

CODE NAME:
★KARMA

136

V

CODE NAME:
★ CARL MARX   K.P.T.
PG.153

★ TURN THE PAGE TO SEE THE WINNER!

S.

137

K.P.T.
PG.151

CODE NAME:
★ DARWIN

138

V

CODE NAME:
★ PESKINESS   K.P.T. PG.152

★ TURN THE PAGE TO SEE THE WINNER!

S.

139

K.P.T.
PG.157

CODE NAME:
★ STICKY

140

V

CODE NAME:
★ PRETTY GIRL

K.P.T.
PG.155

★TURN THE PAGE TO SEE THE WINNER!

S.

141

K.P.T.
PG.151

CODE NAME:
★CAPTAIN MORGAN

142

V

CODE NAME:

★ BARNEY

K.P.T.
PG.156

★ TURN THE PAGE TO SEE THE WINNER!

S.

143

K.P.T.
PP.106–107

CODE NAME:
★ MO

★ BARNEY WINS!

51%

BARNEY

CHEERS, BARNEY!

MO

★ KITTENOLOGICAL CUTEOGRAPHY CHART

CUTEOGRAPHY AND KITTENOLOGY are vast, complex fields that do not lend themselves to easy description, (see page 77) which is probably why scientists and mathematicians couldn't really solve the problem of why kittens are so utterly brilliant. At Kittenwar, however, we are uniquely placed as researchers on the cutting edge of both of these areas of scientific exploration. We have used our extensive knowledge of the field, combined with the most advanced data analysis technology, to create the definitive graphical guide to the complexities of cuteness and the interactions of adorability with the activities of kittens. We do not feel that we are going too far when we suggest that the following flow chart on pages 146–147 will resolve, once and for all, the many questions and uncertainties surrounding the field of cuteness studies.

TURN THE PAGE TO VIEW THE KITTENOLOGICAL CUTEOGRAPHY CHART.

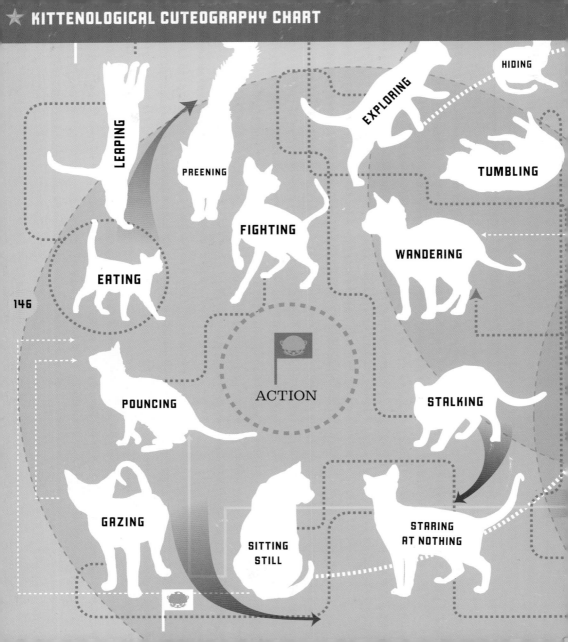

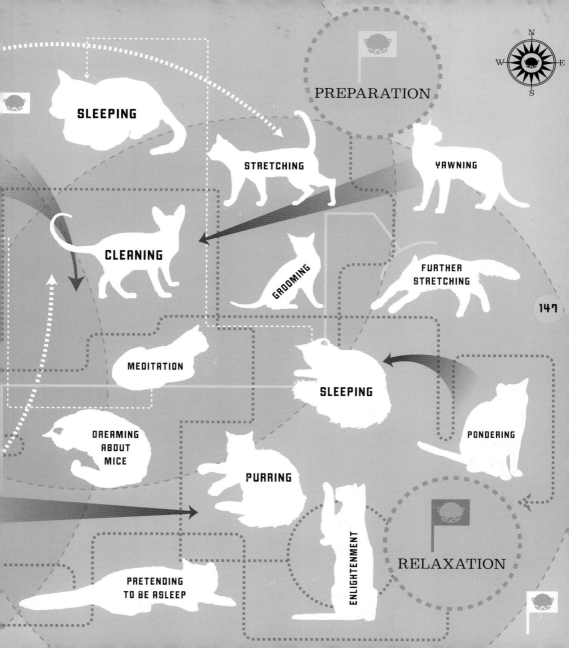

SLEEPING

PREPARATION

STRETCHING

YAWNING

CLEANING

GROOMING

FURTHER
STRETCHING

147

MEDITATION

SLEEPING

PONDERING

DREAMING
ABOUT
MICE

PURRING

ENLIGHTENMENT

RELAXATION

PRETENDING
TO BE ASLEEP

★ KITTENWAR: ARMISTICE

CONGRATULATIONS. You've reached the end of the book. We hope it's been an interesting journey, and that you've learned a little about yourself along the way. Most of all, though, we just hope you've enjoyed the kittens.

When we started Kittenwar, we had no idea of the impact it would have on our lives. We're now perceived as experts in the field of kittenology, called upon by the BBC to give our views on government pet-safety guidelines. We've even been featured on national T.V. in the United States, with a parallel being drawn between a pair of feisty felines on the site and the race for the Senate in Connecticut. Our families and colleagues have come to question our sanity. Best of all, though, we got to write a book.

And what have we learned? Plenty!

⭐ TOP TEN THINGS THAT KITTENWAR HAS TAUGHT US: ⭐

10. NOT ALL WAR IS BAD. A war with kittens in it, for instance, can be great.

9. KITTENS ARE THERAPEUTIC. Gazing at kitty pictures is scientifically proven to be highly beneficial for mental well-being. In fact, we reckon there's a fortune to be made from setting up a nationwide chain of clinics, so that those troubled by the stress of modern life can receive full-contact kitten therapy.

8. KITTENS THAT PRETEND TO BE HUMAN—by standing on their hind legs or learning to operate heavy machinery, for example—are perceived as being cuter than those who insist on retaining their miniature cat personae. We cannot explain this.

7. HUMANS THAT PRETEND TO BE KITTENS—by using a litter box instead of the bathroom or by licking themselves instead of using soap, for example—are probably of unsound mind and in need of urgent kitten therapy (see point 9).

6. PEOPLE WHO LOVE KITTENS are, on average, six times more likely to be successful in life as those who don't. They also have much higher IQs, better jobs, more attractive partners, get fewer parking tickets, and live in nicer houses than non-kitten-loving people.

5. KITTENS ARE BETTER THAN PUPPIES. We don't even have to prove this: it's just a fact. Accept it.

4. LIKE THE OLD CHINESE PROVERB SAYS: give a kitten a fish and you feed him for a day. Teach a kitten to fish and he won't pay any attention at all. So you'll have to give him another fish.

3. IT'S MUCH BETTER TO BE NICE THAN NASTY. And kittens are nice.

2. THERE'S NOT A SINGLE SITUATION in life that can't be improved by the addition of kittens. Not one.

1. ALL OUR KITTENS ARE WINNERS, REALLY.

CROSS KITTENS

You like cross kittens, kittens who look angry and annoyed.

Just because you selected miffed-looking felines doesn't necessarily mean you're particularly grumpy. In fact, it may suggest the opposite. People who go for peeved-looking kitties often choose them because they're feeling sympathy for the plight of those who are facing adversity, while being perfectly happy themselves.

Cross kittens also often have a distinct air of bewilderment about them, and a preference for this indicates a strong desire to help others. Maybe there is someone in your life who needs your assistance in some way; perhaps you could help them with whatever ball of string they've got themselves tangled up in.

Some of our cross kittens look distinctly like they're disapproving of the world in general. If you feel the same way, remember that disapproval doesn't really count for much when you're only six inches tall.

Sometimes people choose angry-looking kitties because they're a little irritated themselves, and their sympathy for fuming felines reflects their own frustrations. If this is the case, you should do as kittens do: pick yourself up, have a quick wash, and act like nothing ever happened. Leave that spilled milk for someone else to clean up.

THIS IS MARSHA, BRILLIANTLY ILLUSTRAT-
ING WHAT A CROSS KITTEN LOOKS LIKE.
MARSHA LIVES IN ENGLAND WITH TOM,
ONE OF THE AUTHORS OF THIS BOOK.

MARSHA

CURIOUS KITTENS

You've chosen curious kittens, the sort of kittens who wander right up to the camera to get a better look, who pick things up in their paws to find out what they do, stick their noses around every door, explore every corner, and generally risk life and whisker to find out as much as they can as fast as possible.

Your choice indicates an inquiring state of mind, open to new experiences and willing to ask the big questions. Now would be a good time to pursue those thoughts and dreams everyone has, to seek new horizons and embrace change.

You might be secretly yearning for travel and adventure. On the other hand, sometimes curiosity doesn't require much movement, and with sufficient imagination and determination, the best discoveries can often be made close to home.

Of course, while it's often a great virtue, everyone knows that curiosity doesn't always agree with cats, so you'd be well advised to take a little care and watch your whiskers the next time something new and intriguing turns up.

151

MARSHA IS VERY CURIOUS ABOUT THE CAMERA. SHE'S CURIOUS ABOUT MOST STUFF, IN FACT, AND REGULARLY SNEAKS INTO PLACES SHE'S NOT ALLOWED TO BE.

MARSHA

PLAYFUL KITTENS

Playful kittens are your first choice in our Kittenwar. Leaping and tumbling, chasing and catching, jumping around or pretending to hunt imaginary mice, these kittens are full of energy and spirit, and you've picked that out as your favorite characteristic.

People like you, who choose bouncing, bubbly kittens, aren't necessarily full of bounce and bubbles, at least outwardly. Kittens, who are naturally overflowing with unselfconscious joy, grow up into dignified and graceful cats who only ever jump when strictly necessary and wouldn't dream of chasing string (well, only on special occasions, or when they think no one is looking).

Like the sensible and intelligent cat, humans should often keep their inner playfulness well hidden. Frivolity and fun rarely impress bank managers or teachers or policemen, and it doesn't do to act kittenish in many situations.

Alternatively, perhaps you have chosen these playful kittens because you don't get enough chances to have fun, in which case you should definitely follow their example and start messing around a bit.

Either way, the fact that you have picked this type of kitten indicates that you understand the importance of play as part of life. You should not allow the necessity of acting like a grown-up to overwhelm the natural impulsiveness and joyfulness that has led you to this choice. Let your inner kitten out to play every once in a while.

MARSHA IS A VERY PLAYFUL KITTEN, AND SHE GOES CRAZY CHASING BALLS OF YARN, BITS OF PAPER, PEOPLE'S FEET, AND THAT GRUMPY OLD BLACK CAT FROM UPSTAIRS.

MARSHA

KITTENS INSIDE STUFF

You've chosen kittens inside stuff. They don't care whether it's a box, a bowl, or a basket, but your favorite felines can't get enough of hiding, sleeping, and playing in things. They're happiest off the floor and in, on, or under something.

In general, kittens who play in and around things are feeling secure and happy in their environment, so your choice could indicate that right now you're happy with where you are and what you're doing. If this is the case, carry on playing in those boxes.

Alternatively, you may have chosen these kittens because you admire their ability to make themselves at home in any situation, to make the best of what life throws at them. Perhaps things aren't going completely according to plan, and you wish you could hide away somewhere small and out of the way.

Kittens don't usually worry about the sorts of things that bother people, and they're big fans of leaping out into the unknown, safe in the knowledge that they will usually land on their feet. A little bit of kittenish bravado will help you deal with your worries and problems. Spend a little less time fretting, a little more messing about, and don't forget to check out interesting new boxes and hiding places—you never know what fun you might find.

153

HIDING IN BOXES IS ONE OF MARSHA'S FAVORITE PASTIMES.

MARSHA

REGULAR CUTE KITTENS

Regular cute kittens are your current favorite: plain, old-fashioned, adorable kittens, without any added flavoring or enhancement. You don't need to see them doing anything, in or on anything, or acting in any particular way. You like them just as they are, in all their simple, straightforward splendor.

It's possible that this choice reflects a yearning for the simpler things in life, and if recent events have been in any way complex or difficult, your affinity for good old-fashioned adorability in kittens is understandable. You should definitely take time to unravel any tangled string lying around the place, and try to keep things neat once you've tidied them up.

Modern life is full of complications, and kittens provide a great contrast to that. All the multifaceted conundrums of the daily world are reduced, in a kitten's eyes, to the question "Can I play with it, eat it, or sleep on it?" You have recognized the great simplicity of this vision in your choice, and should perhaps try to emulate it to attain the peace of mind enjoyed by our feline friends.

THIS WAS QUITE AN EASY PICTURE TO TAKE. MARSHA DOES A VIRTUOSO PERFORMANCE OF "REGULAR CUTE."

MARSHA

SHOUTY KITTENS

You've chosen shouty kittens, kittens who look like they're making a great deal of noise, mouths wide open, meowing for all they're worth. Kittens aren't afraid to raise their voices if they want something, and you might be able to learn from their forthright approach to communication.

If you're not normally a loud person, your choice probably indicates a desire to raise your voice and get yourself noticed. Maybe you've been ignored or overruled one too many times recently, and yelling at people for a change might stop that from happening.

Your choice may also indicate admiration for those who speak up and stand out, and a desire to see that sort of behavior in others. Perhaps someone close to you needs to make themselves heard, but you know that making a big scene isn't really their style. You might even be able to help them out by doing a bit of shouting on their behalf.

Getting your point across isn't always about yelling, though, and you don't always have to raise your voice. Remember, if six inches of kitten can get people running around with a few squeaky mewings, just imagine what a big old human like you could achieve with some carefully considered communication at the appropriate volume.

155

MARSHA DOESN'T ACTUALLY HAVE A VERY LOUD MEOW, BUT SHE TRIES HER BEST, AS YOU CAN SEE.

MARSHA

SLEEPY KITTENS

Sleepy kittens are your number one choice today. Cats are famously good at sleeping and can make themselves completely comfortable in any position, at any time of day; they have an enviable ability to drop off for forty winks on a whim. People don't usually find it quite so easy to get to sleep, and your choice may well indicate that you need to get a bit more rest than you have been recently.

Perhaps life is getting on top of you somewhat, and pictures of snoozing kitties are appealing because you envy their easy, calm restfulness. You should probably follow our kittens' example and take every opportunity to slow down and unwind that presents itself. Kittens don't stay cute unless they get their twenty-odd hours of beauty sleep every day. Try taking catnaps or just staying in bed a little longer than normal.

If you're a naturally relaxed sort of person, your choice might indicate that someone you know needs to unwind a little. In this case you should use your already laid-back feline tendencies to show them the way to the human equivalent of purring, sleepy contentment.

Cats are great at relaxing and letting the world carry on its crazy way while they sit back and relax; we people would benefit from following their example sometimes. Kittens have nine lives' worth of snoozing to get through, but we have just the one—even more reason not to waste time on stress and needless worry.

156

AFTER A LONG DAY CHASING HER OWN TAIL, MARSHA ENJOYS NOTHING MORE THAN A GOOD LONG SNOOZE.

MARSHA

SLIGHTLY ODD KITTENS

They're all cute, but you've chosen our slightly odd kittens over the more normal, classically cute ones; you seem to prefer something a bit different from the norm, kittens from a little off the beaten track, where there's less traffic and more variety.

Your choice of the rather different feline indicates a desire for the alternative instead of the mainstream, and you may be feeling a little tired of the traditional, straightforward way of life. Perhaps you should seek out more adventurous options; try new things, take risks, buy a new brand of cat food.

Many of our more unusual looking kittens look that way because they're actually extremely classy, pedigree animals, with a rich heritage and a family tree that would terrify royalty. In fact, some of them probably are royalty. Maybe you've recognized this, and have chosen them over more down-to-earth kitties because you value history and nobility.

Whatever your reason, you're clearly in the mood for people who stand out from the crowd, and you probably aren't afraid to look a little different yourself. This admirable attitude toward variety is reflected by felines the world over: kittens don't care what their playmates look like, or where they come from; if you can chase yarn with all the others, they really don't mind how strange you look.

157

ONE THING THAT MARSHA CAN'T DO SO EASILY IS LOOK WEIRD, SO WE HAD TO TAKE LOADS OF PICTURES JUST TO GET HER TO PULL A FUNNY FACE.

MARSHA

DEDICATION AND ACKNOWLEDGMENTS

This book is dedicated to Tilly, Bailey, Deeley and Stevens, Marsha, Tim, Sam, and Kapiti.

MANY THANKS to Antony Topping, Ellie Glason, and Nick Harrop at Greene & Heaton; Daniel Greenberg and Monika Verma at Levine Greenberg; Matt Robinson, Beth Steiner, Doug Ogan, Evan Hulka, Leigh Anna McFadden, Kim Romero, Christine Carswell, and Michael Morris at Chronicle Books in San Francisco; Judith Longman and all at Hodder & Stoughton in London; John Yates; Denise Wilton (www.styledeficit.com); Sue Mearns and Jean Gordon; Julie at Comfycatz (www.comfycatzcattery.co.uk); Rob Manuel and the frisky b4ta felines; Giles Littleford and the Labgenius losers; Stephen Colbert; Asia Carrera; Dutchman Dave Roozendaal; Rob Ainsley; the mystery doctor lady; our families; and all Kittenwar users.

Special thanks to Helen Ryan.

PHOTOGRAPHY CREDITS

Extra-special thanks to all those who provided photographs for this book: Kate Abel; David and Laura Alsop; April; Autumn Bagley; Joyce Bess; Brandon Bischof; Stuart Black; Craig and Jayne Brown; Kelly Brown; Annie Burke; Joon and Lauren Chattigré; The Cooper Family; Caroline Cro Costi; Jason Cuddy; Roger, Lisa, Mackenzie, and Colby Dearing; Katherine de Tolly; Renée Faubert; Rae Franklin; Karl Frinkle; Jane Gaylor; Bekki Welter Griffin; Erik and Lisa Griffith; Catherine Griffiths; Gina Guarnieri; Liz Hall; Georgia Hamer; Tania Hennessy and Peter Green; Belén Herrera; Angela Horbatch; Jim and Laura Kane; George and Karen Karyczak; Abby Kenney; Stacey Kinsey; Barbara Klomp; Amy Kohlmyer; Matiss Krastins; Victoria Lane; Chrissie Lange; Leanne Lee; Ravyn Lee; Katie Matheson and Louise Stephens; Petar Mateiasevich; Claire McStravick; Daniel Michaeloff; Luke Minors; Shin and Izumi Morishige; Melinda O'Malley; JoBeth Pan; Jennifer Perry; Kandi Perry; Andrya and Steve Prescott; Amy Procter and Scott Stead; LeAnna Quartuccio; Sole Riley; Alex Roberts; J. Mike Rollins; Amanda Lyn Rowan and Derek Calabro; Charlene Russell and Scott Pinto; Martin T. Sandsmark; Jennifer Schafhauser; Gail B. Schlack; Art and Kathleen Schubert; Chris and Jen Schwerdt; Macy and Hallie Sherwood; Maryann Shirley; Yumiko Soiseth; Christina Tours; Susan Vasconcelos; Oana Vonu-Boriceanu; Helen Whittaker; Natalie Wiggins; Larkin Willis; Kevin and Petra Yahn; Natalie C. Yarbrough; Susan Yee; Liz Zylstra; and all the other Kittenwar photographers.

VINCAT PULCHERRIMUS CATUS JUVENIS